Garfield at large

BY: JIM DAVIS

BALLANTINE BOOKS · NEW YORK

P9-DMT-586

COPYRIGHT© 1980 BY UNITED FEATURE SYNDICATE, INC.

ALL RIGHTS RESERVED UNDER INTERNATIONAL AND PAN-AMERICAN COPYRIGHT
CONVENTIONS. PUBLISHED IN THE UNITED STATES BY BALLANTINE BOOKS,
A DIVISION OF RANDOM HOUSE, INC., NEW YORK, AND SIMULTANEOUSLY IN CANADA
BY RANDOM HOUSE OF CANADA, LIMITED, TORONTO, CANADA.

LIBRARY OF CONGRESS CATALOG CARD NUMBER: 79-93191

ISBN 0-345-28779-7

MANUFACTURED IN THE UNITED STATES OF AMERICA

FIRST EDITION: MARCH 1980

30 29 28 27 26 25 24 23 22 21

LOOK INSIDE THIS BOOK AND SEE THIS CAT...
- EAT LASAGNA
- CHASE DOGS
- DESTROY A MAILMAN
- LAUGH; CRY, FFFT
- SHRED HIS OWNER
- AND MUCH, MUCH MORE!

© 1978 United Feature Syndicate, Inc.

PURRR

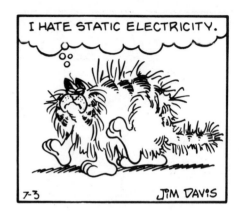

I HATE STATIC ELECTRICITY.

7-3 JIM DAVIS

I REALLY SHOULDN'T EAT THAT FISH...

7-4

© 1978 United Feature Syndicate, Inc. JIM DAVIS

CALL IT AN ETHNIC WEAKNESS.

© 1978 United Feature Syndicate, Inc.

AH, A CURTAIN UPON WHICH TO SHARPEN MY CLAWS.

I HATE DOUBLE-KNIT.

© 1978 United Feature Syndicate, Inc.   7-7

JIM DAVIS

DEAR GARFIELD:
BELIEVE IT OR NOT, I AM AN UGLY KITTEN! OH, I DO ALL THE THINGS "CUTE" KITTENS DO...PLAY WITH YARN AND SUCH, BUT I DON'T GET ANY ATTENTION. WHAT CAN I DO?

MUD FENCE

DEAR "MUD":
YOU'RE TRYING TOO HARD TO BE CUTE. YOU'LL GET MORE ATTENTION IF YOU JUST BE YOURSELF...

7-8

AND SHARPEN YOUR CLAWS ON THE LIVING ROOM DRAPES.

JIM DAVIS   © 1978 United Feature Syndicate, Inc.

POOMP!

7-9

© 1978 United Feature Syndicate, Inc.

7/23

BEWARE OF CAT!

SQUIRT!

7-26 JIM DAVIS

CHUNK
CHUNK
CHUNK
CHUNK
CHUNK
CHUNK
CHUNK
CHUNK

GARFIELD, YOU SHOULD REALLY LEARN TO CONTROL YOUR TEMPER

© 1978 United Feature Syndicate, Inc.

© 1978 United Feature Syndicate, Inc.

NOW WHERE COULD MY PIPE BE?

GARFIELD!!

7-27 JIM DAVIS

DON'T TRY LOOKING CUTE AT ME, GARFIELD. YOU STILL CAN'T HAVE ANY OF MY STEAK.

7-30

© 1978 United Feature Syndicate, Inc.

JIM DAVIS

7-31 © 1978 United Feature Syndicate, Inc.

© 1978 United Feature Syndicate, Inc. 8-1

COME ON, GARFIELD. SNAP OUT OF THIS DEEP BLUE FUNK. SO WHAT IF A DOG MOVED IN...

YOU CAN HANDLE IT. CHEER UP.

8-9

© 1978 United Feature Syndicate, Inc.

TAKE ME NOW, LORD!

JIM DAVIS

WHAT'S YOUR DOG'S NAME?

ODIE

8-10

© 1978 United Feature Syndicate, Inc.

ODIE... A DOG NAMED ODIE...

A BLIMP NAMED HINDENBURG. A SHIP NAMED TITANIC. A CAR NAMED EDSEL. A DOG NAMED...

JIM DAVIS

CRASH!

TEN BILLION DOGS IN THIS WORLD, AND I GET TWEEDLEE THE WONDER DUMMY.

8-11 JIM DAVIS

WOOF!

BARK!

YIP! YIP! YIP! YIP!

JIM DAVIS

POOR ME.

SIGH...A BIG, VICIOUS, BRUTE OF A DOG HAS MOVED INTO MY HOME...

GRAB!

WHAP
WHAP
WHAP
WHAP
WHAP
WHAP
WHAP

DRIBBLE
DRIBBLE
DRIBBLE

© 1978 United Feature Syndicate, Inc

8-13

PUNT

HOW WILL I EVER SURVIVE?

JIM DAVIS

WE CATS ARE THE SOURCE OF MANY MYTHS...

THE SAYING, "NERVOUS AS A CAT", IS AN OLD WIVE'S TALE.

8-20

BARK!

NOT TO MENTION, "A CAT ALWAYS LANDS ON HIS FEET".

JIM DAVIS

HEH, HEH, HEH

SPLASH SPLASH SPLASH

© 1978 United Feature Syndicate, Inc.

CATS JUST LOVE TO PLAY WITH WATER

JIM DAVIS

WHEW! I THOUGHT I'D NEVER FIND JON'S WATCH

8-21

DAB DAB DAB DAB

© 1978 United Feature Syndicate, Inc.   JIM DAVIS

SPLASH! SPLASH! SPLASH SPLASH! SPLASH!

MY CHICKEN SOUP!

THE DEVIL MADE ME DO IT

8-22

© 1978 United Feature Syndicate, Inc.

JIM DAVIS

8-25

© 1978 United Feature Syndicate, Inc.

SPLOOCH!

8-26

HELP YOURSELF TO THE LASAGNA, GARFIELD.

JIM DAVIS

GARFIELD, AS OF THIS MINUTE, I'M PUTTING YOU ON A DIET

8-28 © 1978 United Feature Syndicate, Inc.

GARFIELD?

I THINK I SNAPPED HIS MIND

JIM DAVIS

COME ON, OLD BUDDY. GOING ON A DIET'S NOT ALL THAT BAD. WHY, A COUPLE OF POUNDS OFF THE MIDDLE AND YOU'LL BE FIT AND TRIM AGAIN

8-29 © 1978 United Feature Syndicate, Inc.

THAT'S BETTER

JIM DAVIS

I DIDN'T HAVE THE HEART TO TELL HIM HE'S MADE THE WEIGHT WATCHER'S TEN MOST-WANTED LIST

9-6

© 1978 United Feature Syndicate, Inc.

JIM DAVIS

HEE-HEE-HEE

© 1978 United Feature Syndicate, Inc.

9-7

HA-HA-HA-HA-HA

JIM DAVIS

AND THAT'S ALL FOR MYSTERY THEATER. ...GOOD 'NIGHT.

© 1978 United Feature Syndicate, Inc.

CLICK!

GARFIELD! CUT THAT OUT!

CLICK!

9-8 JIM DAVIS

WHAT'RE YOU DOING TONIGHT, LYMAN?

I'M GONNA CATCH THE NEW FLICK DOWN AT THE BIJOU.

© 1978 United Feature Syndicate, Inc.

9-9

IT'S ABOUT THIS KID WHO PUTS A TACK IN HIS TEACHER'S CHAIR, AND SHE SITS ON IT.

NOT MUCH OF A PLOT.

I SUPPOSE NOT. BUT I STILL ENJOY THE MOVIES WHERE THE BOY GETS THE GIRL IN THE END.

JIM DAVIS

9-11

© 1978 United Feature Syndicate, Inc.

★◑✦// LEG CRAMPS

JIM DAVIS

HMMMMM

9-12

SMACK!

© 1978 United Feature Syndicate, Inc.

JIM DAVIS

JIM DAVIS

© 1978 United Feature Syndicate, Inc.

SLAM!

9-17

VETERINARY CLINIC

SOMEHOW, THEY ALWAYS KNOW.

SCRATCH
SCRATCH
SCRATCH
SCRATCH
SCRATCH
SCRATCH
SCRATCH
SCRATCH
SCRATCH
SCRATCH
SCRATCH
SCRATCH
SCRATCH
SCRATCH

GOOD MORNING, GARFIELD

TODAY WE'RE GOING TO LEARN TO WALK ON A LEASH

JIM DAVIS

10-8

© 1978 United Feature Syndicate, Inc.

KABONKA BONKA BONKA

ROWRR!

I TELL YOU, THELMA, THIS NEIGHBORHOOD IS GETTING WEIRDER BY THE MINUTE

GARFIELD! I'M BACK FROM THE STORE

WE'RE HAVING A COOKOUT TONIGHT. I GOT STEAK AND CORN AND...

AND YOU JUST ATE THE BRIQUETTES

10-13

JIM DAVIS © 1978 United Feature Syndicate, Inc.

© 1978 United Feature Syndicate, Inc.
10-14

CATS ARE NICE TO HAVE WHEN YOU'RE FEELING LONELY

JIM DAVIS

I TOOK GARFIELD TO THE VET TO BE DECLAWED

© 1978 United Feature Syndicate, Inc.

10·20

THEY'RE REMOVING HIS STITCHES NEXT THURSDAY

POOR GARFIELD

WHO'S TALKING ABOUT GARFIELD?

JIM DAVIS

I'M SORRY I TRIED TO HAVE YOU DECLAWED, GARFIELD

I LOVE YOU JUST THE WAY YOU ARE, CLAWS AND ALL

10·21

© 1978 United Feature Syndicate, Inc.

SOMEDAY, SOMEHOW, WHEN YOU'RE LEAST EXPECTING IT, I'M GOING TO SHRED YOUR BEDROOM SUITE

JIM DAVIS

IT'S THAT TIME OF YEAR AGAIN...

AT HALLOWEEN WE CATS BECOME BEWITCHED...

OUR EYES TURN BLOOD RED...

10-29

OUR FANGS GROW...

AND OUR HAIR STANDS UP.

JIM DAVIS

© 1978 United Feature Syndicate, Inc.

NOT TO MENTION LONGER CLAWS

AAYI EEE!

THAT'S RIGHT, DOC. HE SCREAMED, TURNED WHITE, AND PASSED OUT.

BUZZ
SAW
SAW
SCRATCH
SCRATCH
CUT
CUT
BZZZ

WHY DON'T YOU BOYS GO FIGHT OR SOMETHING?

© 1978 United Feature Syndicate, Inc.

HI, JON!

HI, LYMAN

SLAM!

I'M STARVED! WHAT'S TO EAT?

NOTHING. I'M EATING THE LAST OF THE FOOD

11-12

JIM DAVIS

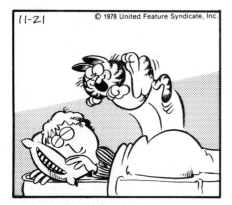

HACK
SNIFF
WHEEZE
SNIFF

© 1978 United Feature Syndicate, Inc.

11-29

GOBBLE!
GOBBLE!
GOBBLE!
GOBBLE!

OR IS IT:
STARVE A COLD,
FEED A FEVER?

JIM DAVIS

AH
AH
AH
AH

GARFIELD

11-30

WAH-CHOO!

BLESS YOU

GARFIELD

SNIFF

JIM DAVIS

© 1978 United Feature Syndicate, Inc.

DO YOU KNOW YOUR CAT'S SITTING ON MY MEAT LOAF?

12-4

NO, BUT IF YOU HUM A COUPLE OF BARS I'LL FAKE IT

© 1978 United Feature Syndicate, Inc.

THIS IS GOING TO BE A LONG WEEK

JIM DAVIS

SEE YOU LATER, GARFIELD. I'M GOING TO THE GROCERY STORE

© 1978 United Feature Syndicate, Inc.

VERY WELL, YOU MAY COME ALONG

12-5 JIM DAVIS

© 1978 United Feature Syndicate, Inc.

© 1978 United Feature Syndicate, Inc.

© 1978 United Feature Syndicate Inc

HERE, ODIE!

12-10

JIM DAVIS

ISN'T IT A LITTLE COLD TO TAKE ODIE FOR A WALK?

NONSENSE!

THINGS TO DO:
1. wash car
2. do laundry

12-11

3. and brush Garfield

© 1978 United Feature Syndicate, Inc.

JIM DAVIS

I OWN A CAT

12-12

© 1978 United Feature Syndicate, Inc.

AND WHEN YOU OWN A CAT, EATING A NORMAL MEAL TAKES ON AN ALL-NEW PERSPECTIVE

KNOWING THAT SOMEWHERE IN THERE IS A CAT HAIR WITH YOUR NAME ON IT

JIM DAVIS

© 1978 United Feature Syndicate, Inc.

12-18 JIM DAVIS

ZZZZZZ.

YAWN!

WHAT A HECK OF A WAY TO WAKE UP

© 1978 United Feature Syndicate, Inc.

12-19

JIM DAVIS

© 1978 United Feature Syndicate, Inc.

I KNOW CATS ARE FAST, BUT **THAT'S** RIDICULOUS

POW!

© 1979 United Feature Syndicate, Inc.

JIM DAVIS

1-1

WHAT WOULD YOU LIKE FOR BREAKFAST, GARFIELD?

A CUP OF COFFEE, A DANISH AND THE NEWSPAPER

© 1979 United Feature Syndicate, Inc.

HAVE A WARM BOWL OF MILK

YOU PEOPLE DON'T GIVE US CATS ANY CREDIT!

JIM DAVIS

1-2

© 1979 United Feature Syndicate, Inc.

1-12

© 1979 United Feature Syndicate, Inc.

1-13

1-15

JIM DAVIS © 1979 United Feature Syndicate, Inc.

GARFIELD, YOU SHOULDN'T CHASE THE MAILMAN LIKE THAT

NOW WHAT WOULD YOU DO WITH HIM IF YOU ACTUALLY CAUGHT HIM?

I'D EAT HIM

GARFIELD, YOU KNOW CATS CAN'T DRINK...

1-16 © 1979 United Feature Syndicate, Inc.

...COFFEE

SLURP!

WELL, I'LL BE DIPPED

FILL'ER UP

JIM DAVIS

IT'S AMAZING HOW WE'VE GROWN TO UNDERSTAND ONE ANOTHER

1-17

LOOK, GARFIELD. A MOUSE!

1-18

EEEK!

SCRATCH
SCRATCH
SCRATCH
SCRATCH

UH-OH.
FLEAS!

ALCOHOL SHOULD DO THE TRICK

MUCH BETTER

PUFF
PUFF

1979 United Feature Syndicate, Inc.

FOOMP

THERE'S SOMETHING TO BE SAID FOR FLEA COLLARS

JIM DAVIS

1-21